STOMP, WIGGLE, CLAP, AND TAP

MY FIRST BOOK OF DANCE

RACHELLE BURK

Illustrated by Alyssa De Asis

ROCKRIDGE PRESS

For Cara, my dancing girl

For general information on our other products and services, please contact our Customer Care Department within the United States at (866) 744-2665, or outside the United States at (510) 253-0500.

Hardcover ISBN: 979-8-88608-528-0
Paperback ISBN: 978-1-64876-838-5
eBook ISBN: 978-1-64876-257-4

Manufactured in the United States of America

Interior and Cover Designer: Tricia Jang
Art Producer: Sara Feinstein
Editor: Elizabeth Baird
Production Editor: Nora Milman
Production Manager: Martin Worthington

Illustration © 2021 Alyssa De Asis.
Author photo courtesy of Alana Barouch.

10 9 8 7 6 5 4 3 2 1 0

A Note to Caregivers

Dance has been called "the hidden language of the soul," and was one of the earliest forms of communication. For thousands of years, it has been used across all cultures to celebrate, tell stories, entertain, and perform rituals.

Toddlers are little motion machines. They love to dance and will naturally start moving to music between 15 and 20 months of age. Dance has many benefits, helping your child develop balance, coordination, and control. It stimulates the brain and provides a fun, creative way to channel their energy and build self-confidence.

You can encourage your toddler by playing music they enjoy and providing simple instruments that they can shake or bang. Toddlers will imitate what they see. Use this book to introduce your child to dance, with body movements that get progressively more complex as the book goes along. For children with physical or developmental disabilities, movements can be adapted to accommodate individual needs. The first part of the book will instruct them to isolate individual body parts, like their hands, arms, and legs, building spatial awareness and gross motor skills. The second will have them use their whole bodies, giving them plenty of chances to get their wiggles out. Dance along with them!

Hello, friend! It's time to **dance**.
Twirl and wiggle, hop and prance.
Turn on music, sing a song,
let your body move along.

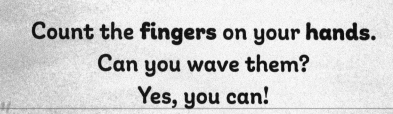

Count the **fingers** on your **hands**.
Can you wave them?
Yes, you can!

Wave hello and
wave goodbye.

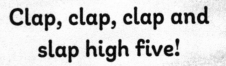

Clap, clap, clap and
slap high five!

Sleeping fingers, curled in tight.
Watch them rise in morning light.

Shut them, open, shake, shake, shake,
little fingers wide-awake.

Raise your arms up, left and right.
Move them like a bird in flight.
Drop them down, then lift them high,
flap, flap, birdie in the sky!

You are in a marching band,
wooden drumstick in each hand.
Bend your arms and beat that drum,
rat-a-tat and rum-tum-tum!

Twirl your arms like two big wheels,
round and round—how does it feel?

Left turn, right turn, vroom, vroom, vroom!
Faster, faster, zoom, zoom, zoom!

Hands together, bend down low.
Elephant trunk sways to and fro.

Lift your trunk up off the ground
and spray water all around!

Now move your **legs**—you have a pair!
They stomp and kick and climb up stairs.
One step, two steps, three steps, four—
Soon you're walking out the door!

Stand up tall and spread your feet.
Bend your **knees** to take a seat.

Once again, spring way up tall.
Up, down, up, down, bouncy ball!

Hippity, hoppity, dancing frog,
jump along from log to log.

Leap at a fly, and in a flash,
land in the water and make a splash!

Sit right down,
it's time to meet
ten squiggle **toes**
on two little **feet**.

Forward bend, touch knees to nose.
Reach and grab those squiggle toes.

On your **tiptoes**, spin, spin, spin!
Stretch your arms, turn in the wind.

Round and round the pinwheel goes,
every time the cool wind blows.

Prancing pony round the track,
stomping hooves go clop-clop-clack.
Jump a fence, then give a neigh.
One more jump, then trot away.

Swing your **hips** in a big wide loop.
Whirl and twirl your Hula-Hoop.

Swing those hips the other way.
You can hula every day!

All together, here's your chance.
Move your **whole self** in a dance!
Top to bottom, bounce and jiggle,
slide and glide until you giggle.

Shake your **body** all about.
Poke your little backside out.

Wiggle down and wiggle up,
wag your tail like a happy pup!

Slooowly stretch on tippy-toes.
This is how the tall tree grows.
Swing your arms round every way.
This is how the branches sway.

Squeeze your hands into a bunch.
Left-right-left-right, ninja punch!

Swing each leg up very quick.
Left-right-left-right, ninja kick!

Tuck your hands
beneath your arms.
Flap like chickens
on the farm.

Strut about on chicken legs.
Squat to sit upon your eggs.

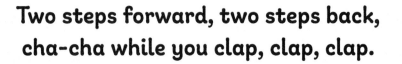

Two steps forward, two steps back,
cha-cha while you clap, clap, clap.

Two steps left, then two steps right,
cha-cha-cha all day and night.

Dancing friend, it's time to show everyone those moves you know.

Clapping hands to tapping feet,
rock and roll to your own beat.

Resources

Websites

* Mom Loves Best: "Benefits of Dance for Kids"
  MomLovesBest.com/benefits-of-dance-for-kids

Videos

* The Wiggles Channel
  Toddler music and dance with The Wiggles and costumed characters
  YouTube.com/TheWiggles

* Bounce Patrol
  Songs and nursery rhymes to get children up and bouncing, with Spanish-language selections
  YouTube.com/BouncePatrolKids

* The Learning Station
  Music and movement (including ESL selections) for ages 1 to 10
  YouTube.com/TheLearningStation

* Daniella Ballerina
  The perfect place for little ballerinas to begin their adventure in the world of ballet
  YouTube.com/DaniellaBallerina

* **Ready Set Dance**
  Australian dance company channel for preschoolers to practice at home
  YouTube.com/ReadySetDance

* **Zumbini Time**
  Zumba fitness program of music and dance for toddlers
  YouTube.com/Zumbini

* **SamCam's Dance Studio**
  Dance videos for toddlers and older children, provided by a professional instructor
  YouTube.com/SamCamsCreations

About the Author

RACHELLE BURK writes fiction and nonfiction for children ages 3 to 13. Picture books include: *Don't Turn the Page!*, *Tree House in a Storm*, *The Best Four Questions*, and the award-winning biography *Painting in the Dark: Esref Armagan, Blind Artist*. Chapter books include: *The Story of Simone Biles* (a Rockridge Press biography) and *The Tooth Fairy Trap* (a One School, One Book selection). She also wrote a science-adventure novel: *The Walking Fish* (winner of the National Science Teachers Association & Children's Book Council award). Rachelle has written for numerous children's magazines, including *Scholastic Science World*, *Scholastic SuperScience*, *Scholastic Scope*, and *Highlights*. She is the founder of the writers' resource site ResourcesforChildrensWriters.com. A retired social worker, Rachelle is also a children's entertainer, performing as Tickles the Clown and Mother Goof Storyteller. When she's not writing, Rachelle enjoys adventure travel, scuba diving, hiking, and caving. You can find out more about her books and school visits at RachelleBurk.com.

About the Illustrator

Combining elements from nature with vibrant colors and whimsical characters and settings, Filipino artist ALYSSA DE ASIS crafts illustrations with a unique, lighthearted feel to them. She's a natural when it comes to children's illustration, but her style also suits editorial, fashion, and publishing projects.